Dust of the Desert

Lyman D. Hinckley

Alpha Editions

This edition published in 2021

ISBN : 9789355395474

Design and Setting By
Alpha Editions
www.alphaedis.com
Email - info@alphaedis.com

DUST UNTO DUST

Martin set the lifeboat down carefully, with all the attention one usually exercises in a situation where the totally unexpected has occurred, and he and his two companions sat and stared in awed silence at the city a quarter-mile away.

He saw the dull, black walls of buildings shouldering grimly into the twilight sky, saw the sheared edge where the metal city ended and the barren earth began ... and he remembered observing, even before they landed, the too-strict geometry imposed on the entire construction.

He frowned. The first impression was ... malignant.

Wass, blond and slight, with enough nose for three or four men, unbuckled his safety belt and stood up. "Shall we, gentlemen?" and with a graceful movement of hand and arm he indicated the waiting city.

Martin led Wass, and the gangling, scarecrow-like Rodney, through the stillness overlaying the barren ground. There was only the twilight sky, and harsh and black against it, the convoluted earth. And the city. Malignant. He wondered, again, what beings would choose to build a city—even a city like this one—in such surroundings.

The men from the ship knew only the surface facts about this waiting geometric discovery. Theirs was the eleventh inter-planetary flight, and the previous ten, in the time allowed them for exploration while this planet was still close enough to their own to permit a safe return in their ships, had not spotted the city. But the eleventh expedition had, an hour ago, with just thirteen hours left during which a return flight could be safely started. So far as was known, this was the only city on the planet—the planet without any life at all, save tiny mosses, for a million years or more. And no matter which direction from the city a man moved, he would always be going north.

"Hey, Martin!" Rodney called through his helmet radio. Martin paused. "Wind," Rodney said, coming abreast of him. He glanced toward the black pile, as if sharing Martin's thoughts. "That's all we need, isn't it?"

Martin looked at the semi-transparent figures of wind and dust cavorting in the distance, moving toward them. He grinned a little, adjusting his radio. "Worried?"

Rodney's bony face was without expression. "Gives me the creeps, kind of. I wonder what they were like?"

Wass murmured, "Let us hope they aren't immortal."

Three feet from the edge of the city Martin stopped and stubbed at the sand with the toe of his boot, clearing earth from part of a shining metal band.

Wass watched him, and then shoved aside more sand, several feet away. "It's here, too."

Martin stood up. "Let's try farther on. Rodney, radio the ship, tell them we're going in."

Rodney nodded.

After a time, Wass said, "Here, too. How far do you think it goes?"

Martin shrugged. "Clear around the city? I'd like to know what it is—was—for."

"Defense," Rodney, several yards behind, suggested.

"Could be," Martin said. "Let's go in."

The three crossed the metal band and walked abreast down a street, their broad soft soled boots making no sound on the dull metal. They passed doors and arches and windows and separate buildings. They moved cautiously across five intersections. And they stood in a square surrounded by the tallest buildings in the city.

Rodney broke the silence, hesitantly. "Not—not very big. Is it?"

Wass looked at him shrewdly. "Neither were the—well, shall we call them, people? Have you noticed how low everything is?"

Rodney's laughter rose, too. Then, sobering—"Maybe they crawled."

A nebulous image, product of childhood's vivid imagination, moved slowly across Martin's mind. "All right!" he rapped out—and the image faded.

"Sorry," Rodney murmured, his throat working beneath his lantern jaw. Then—"I wonder what it's like here in the winter when there's no light at all?"

"I imagine they had illumination of some sort," Martin answered, dryly. "If we don't hurry up and get through this place and back to the ship, we're very likely to find out."

Rodney said quickly, "I mean outside."

"Out there, too, Rodney, they must have had illumination." Martin looked back along the straight, metal street they'd walked on, and past that out over the bleak, furrowed slopes where the ship's lifeboat lay ... and he thought everything outside the city seemed, somehow, from here, a little dim, a little hazy.

He straightened his shoulders. The city was alien, of course, and that explained most of it ... most of it. But he felt the black city was something familiar, yet twisted and distorted.

"Well," Wass said, his nose wrinkling a bit, "now that we're here...."

"Pictures," Martin decided. "We have twelve hours. We'll start here. What's the matter, Wass?"

The blond man grinned ruefully. "I left the camera in the lifeboat." There was a pause. Then Wass, defensively—"It's almost as if the city didn't want to be photographed."

Martin ignored the remark. "Go get it. Rodney and I will be somewhere along this street."

Wass turned away. Martin and Rodney started slowly down the wide metal street, at right angles to their path of entrance.

Again Martin felt a tug of twisted, distorted familiarity. It was almost as if ... they were human up to a certain point, the point being, perhaps, some part of their minds.... Alien things, dark and subtle, things no man could ever comprehend.

Parallel evolution on two inner planets of the same system? Somewhere, sometime, a common ancestor? Martin noted the shoulder-high doors, the heavier gravity, remembered the inhabitants of the city vanished before the thing that was to become man ever emerged from the slime, and he decided to grin at himself, at his own imagination.

Rodney jerked his scarecrow length about quickly, and a chill sped up Martin's spine. "What's the matter?"

The bony face was white, the gray eyes were wide. "I saw—I thought I saw—something—moving—"

Anger rose in Martin. "You didn't," he said flatly, gripping the other's shoulder cruelly. "You couldn't have. Get hold of yourself, man!"

Rodney stared. "The wind. Remember? There isn't any, here."

"... How could there be? The buildings protect us now. It was blowing from the other direction."

Rodney wrenched free of Martin's grip. He gestured wildly. "That—"

"Martin!" Wass' voice came through the receivers in both their radios. "Martin, I can't get out!"

Rodney mumbled something, and Martin told him to shut up.

Wass said, more quietly, "Remember that metal band? It's all clear now, and glittering, as far as I can see. I can't get across it; it's like a glass wall."

"We're trapped, we're trapped, they are—"

"Shut up, Rodney! Wass, I'm only two sections from the edge. I'll check here."

Martin clapped a hand on Rodney's shoulder again, starting him moving, toward the city's edge, past the black, silent buildings.

The glittering band was here, too, like a halo around a silhouette.

"No go," Martin said to Wass. He bit at his lower lip. "I think it must be all around us." He was silent for a time, exploring the consequences of this. Then—"We'll meet you in the middle of the city, where we separated."

Walking with Rodney, Martin heard Wass' voice, flat and metallic through the radio receiver against his ear. "What do you suppose caused this?"

He shook his head angrily, saying, "Judging by reports of the rest of the planet, it must have been horribly radioactive at one time. All of it."

"Man-made radiation, you mean."

Martin grinned faintly. Wass, too, had an active imagination. "Well, alien-made, anyhow. Perhaps they had a war."

Wass' voice sounded startled. "Anti-radiation screen?"

Rodney interrupted, "There hasn't been enough radiation around here for hundreds of thousands of years to activate such a screen."

Wass said coldly, "He's right, Martin."

Martin crossed an intersection, Rodney slightly behind him. "You're both wrong," he said. "We landed here today."

Rodney stopped in the middle of the metal street and stared down at Martin. "The wind—?"

"Why not?"

"That would explain why it stopped so suddenly, then." Rodney stood straighter. When he walked again, his steps were firmer.

They reached the center of the city, ahead of the small, slight Wass, and stood watching him labor along the metal toward them.

Wass' face, Martin saw, was sober. "I tried to call the ship. No luck."

"The shield?"

Wass nodded. "What else?"

"I don't know—"

"If we went to the roof of the tallest building," Rodney offered, "we might—"

Martin shook his head. "No. To be effective, the shield would have to cover the city."

Wass stared down at the metal street, as if he could look through it. "I wonder where it gets its power?"

"Down below, probably. If there is a down below." Martin hesitated. "We may have to...."

"What?" Rodney prompted.

Martin shrugged. "Let's look."

He led the way through a shoulder-high arch in one of the tall buildings surrounding the square. The corridor inside was dim and plain, and he switched on his flashlight, the other two immediately following his example. The walls and the rounded ceiling of the corridor were of the same dull metal as the buildings' facades, and the streets. There were a multitude of doors and arches set into either side of the corridor.

It was rather like ... entering a gigantic metal beehive.

Martin chose an arch, with beyond it a metal ramp, which tilted downward, gleaming in the pale circle of his torch.

A call from Rodney halted him. "Back here," the tall man repeated. "It looks like a switchboard."

The three advanced to the end of the central corridor, pausing before a great arch, outlined in the too-careful geometrical figures Martin had come to associate with the city builders. The three torches, shining through the arch, picked out a bank of buttons, handles ... and a thick rope of cables which ran upward to vanish unexpectedly in the metal roof.

"Is this it," Wass murmured, "or an auxiliary?"

Martin shrugged. "The whole city's no more than a machine, apparently."

"Another assumption," Wass said. "We have done nothing but make assumptions ever since we got here."

"What would you suggest, instead?" Martin asked calmly.

Rodney furtively, extended one hand toward a switch.

"No!" Martin said, sharply. That was one assumption they dared not make.

Rodney turned. "But—"

"No. Wass, how much time have we?"

"The ship leaves in eleven hours."

"Eleven hours," Rodney repeated. "Eleven hours!" He reached out for the switch again. Martin swore, stepped forward, pulled him back roughly.

He directed his flashlight at Rodney's thin, pale face. "What do you think you're doing?"

"We have to find out what all this stuff's for!"

"Going at it blindly, we'd probably execute ourselves."

"We've got to—"

"No!" Then, more quietly—"We still have eleven hours to find a way out."

"Ten hours and forty-five minutes," Wass disagreed softly. "Minus the time it takes us to get to the lifeboat, fly to the ship, land, stow it, get ourselves aboard, and get the big ship away from the planet. And Captain Morgan can't wait for us, Martin."

"You too, Wass?"

"Up to the point of accuracy, yes."

Martin said, "Not necessarily. You go the way the wind does, always thinking of your own tender hide, of course."

Rodney cursed. "And every second we stand here doing nothing gives us that much less time to find a way out. Martin—"

"Make one move toward that switchboard and I'll stop you where you stand!"

Wass moved silently through the darkness beyond the torches. "We all have guns, Martin."

"I'm holding mine." Martin waited.

After a moment, Wass switched his flashlight back on. He said quietly, "He's right, Rodney. It would be sure death to monkey around in here."

"Well...." Rodney turned quickly toward the black arch. "Let's get out of here, then!"

Martin hung back waiting for the others to go ahead of him down the metal hall. At the other arch, where the ramp led downward, he called a halt. "If the dome, or whatever it is, is a radiation screen there must be at least half-a-dozen emergency exits around the city."

Rodney said, "To search every building next to the dome clean around the city would take years."

Martin nodded. "But there must be central roads beneath this main level leading to them. Up here there are too many roads."

Wass laughed rudely.

"Have you a better idea?"

Wass ignored that, as Martin hoped he would. He said slowly, "That leads to another idea. If the band around the city is responsible for the dome, does it project down into the ground as well?"

"You mean *dig* out?" Martin asked.

"Sure. Why not?"

"We're wearing heavy suits and bulky breathing units. We have no equipment."

"That shouldn't be hard to come by."

Martin smiled, banishing Wass' idea.

Rodney said, "They may have had their digging equipment built right in to themselves."

"Anyway," Martin decided, "we can take a look down below."

"In the pitch dark," Wass added.

Martin adjusted his torch, began to lead the way down the metal ramp. The incline was gentle, apparently constructed for legs shorter, feet perhaps less broad than their own. The metal, without mark of any sort, gleamed under the combined light of the torches, unrolling out of the darkness before the men.

At length the incline melted smoothly into the next level of the city.

Martin shined his light upward, and the others followed his example. Metal as smooth and featureless as that on which they stood shone down on them.

Wass turned his light parallel with the floor, and then moved slowly in a circle. "No supports. No supports anywhere. What keeps all that up there?"

"I don't know. I have no idea." Martin gestured toward the ramp with his light. "Does all this, this whole place, look at all familiar to you?"

Rodney's gulp was clearly audible through the radio receivers. "Here?"

"No, no," Martin answered impatiently, "not just here. I mean the whole city."

"Yes," Wass said dryly, "it does. I'm sure this is where all my nightmares stay when they're not on shift."

Martin turned on his heel and started down a metal avenue which, he thought, paralleled the street above. And Rodney and Wass followed him silently. They moved along the metal, past unfamiliar shapes made more so by gloom and moving shadows, past doors dancing grotesquely in the three lights, past openings in the occasional high metal partitions, past something which was perhaps a conveyor belt, past another something which could have been anything at all.

The metal street ended eventually in a blank metal wall.

The edge of the city—the city which was a dome of force above and a bowl of metal below.

After a long time, Wass sighed. "Well, skipper...?"

"We go back, I guess," Martin said.

Rodney turned swiftly to face him. Martin thought the tall man was holding his gun. "To the switchboard, Martin?"

"Unless someone has a better idea," Martin conceded. He waited. But Rodney was holding the gun ... and Wass was.... Then—"I can't think of anything else."

They began to retrace their steps along the metal street, back past the same dancing shapes of metal, the partitions, the odd windows, all looking different now in the new angles of illumination.

Martin was in the lead. Wass followed him silently. Rodney, tall, matchstick thin, even in his cumbersome suit, swayed with jaunty triumph in the rear.

Martin looked at the metal street lined with its metal objects and he sighed. He remembered how the dark buildings of the city looked at surface level, how the city itself looked when they were landing, and then when they were walking toward it. The dream was gone again for now. Idealism died in him, again and again, yet it was always reborn. But—The only city, so far as anyone knew, on the first planet they'd ever explored. And it had to be like this. Nightmares, Wass said, and Martin thought perhaps the city was built by a race of beings who at some point twisted away from their evolutionary spiral, plagued by a sort of racial insanity.

No, Martin thought, shaking his head. No, that couldn't be. Viewpoint ... his viewpoint. It was the haunting sense of familiarity, a faint strain through all this broad jumble, the junkpile of alien metal, which was making him theorize so wildly.

Then Wass touched his elbow. "Look there, Martin. Left of the ramp."

Light from their torches was reflected, as from glass.

"All right," Rodney said belligerently into his radio. "What's holding up the procession?"

Martin was silent.

Wass undertook to explain. Why not, after all? Martin asked himself. It was in Wass' own interest. In a moment, all three were standing before a bank of glass cases which stretched off into the distance as far as the combined light of their torches would reach.

"Seeds!" Wass exclaimed, his faceplate pressed against the glass.

Martin blinked. He thought how little time they had. He wet his lips.

Wass' gloved hands fumbled awkwardly at a catch in the nearest section of the bank.

Martin thought of the dark, convoluted land outside the city. If they wouldn't grow there.... Or had they, once? "Don't, Wass!"

Torchlight reflected from Wass' faceplate as he turned his head. "Why not?"

They were like children.... "We don't know, released, what they'll do."

"Skipper," Wass said carefully, "if we don't get out of this place by the deadline we may be eating these."

Martin raised his arm tensely. "Opening a seed bank doesn't help us find a way out of here." He started up the ramp. "Besides, we've no water."

Rodney came last up the ramp, less jaunty now, but still holding the gun. His mind, too, was taken up with childhood's imaginings. "For a plant to grow in this environment, it wouldn't need much water. Maybe—" he had a vision of evil plants attacking them, growing with super-swiftness at the air valves and joints of their suits "—only the little moisture in the atmosphere."

They stood before the switchboard again. Martin and Wass side by side, Rodney, still holding his gun, slightly to the rear.

Rodney moved forward a little toward the switches. His breathing was loud and rather uneven in the radio receivers.

Martin made a final effort. "Rodney, it's still almost nine hours to take off. Let's search awhile first. Let this be a last resort."

Rodney jerked his head negatively. "No. Now, I know you, Martin. Postpone and postpone until it's too late, and the ship leaves without us and we're stranded here to eat seeds and gradually dehydrate ourselves and God only knows what else and—"

He reached out convulsively and yanked a switch.

Martin leaped, knocking him to the floor. Rodney's gun skittered away silently, like a live thing, out of the range of the torches.

The radio receivers impersonally recorded the grating sounds of Rodney's sobs.

"Sorry," Martin said, without feeling. He turned quickly. "Wass?"

The slight, blond man stood unmoving. "I'm with you, Martin, but, as a last resort it might be better to be blown sky high than to die gradually—"

Martin was watching Rodney, struggling to get up. "I agree. As a last resort. We still have a little time."

Rodney's tall, spare figure looked bowed and tired in the torchlight, now that he was up again. "Martin, I—"

Martin turned his back. "Skip it, Rodney," he said gently.

"Water," Wass said thoughtfully. "There must be reservoirs under this city somewhere."

Rodney said, "How does water help us get out?"

Martin glanced at Wass, then started out of the switchboard room, not looking back. "It got in and out of the city some way. Perhaps we can leave the same way."

Down the ramp again.

"There's another ramp," Wass murmured.

Rodney looked down it. "I wonder how many there are, all told."

Martin placed one foot on the metal incline. He angled his torch down, picking out shadowy, geometrical shapes, duplicates of the ones on the present level. "We'll find out," he said, "how many there are."

Eleven levels later Rodney asked, "How much time have we now?"

"Seven hours," Wass said quietly, "until take-off."

"One more level," Martin said, ignoring the reference to time. "I ... think it's the last."

They walked down the ramp and stood together, silent in a dim pool of artificial light on the bottom level of the alien city.

Rodney played his torch about the metal figures carefully placed about the floor. "Martin, what if there are no reservoirs? What if there are cemeteries instead? Or cold storage units? Maybe the switch I pulled—"

"Rodney! Stop it!"

Rodney swallowed audibly. "This place scares me...."

"The first time I was ever in a rocket, it scared me. I was thirteen."

"This is different," Wass said. "Built-in traps—"

"They had a war," Martin said.

Wass agreed. "And the survivors retired here. Why?"

Martin said, "They wanted to rebuild. Or maybe this was already built before the war as a retreat." He turned impatiently. "How should I know?"

Wass turned, too, persistent. "But the planet was through with them."

"In a minute," Martin said, too irritably, "we'll have a sentient planet." From the corner of his eye he saw Rodney start at that. "Knock it off, Wass. We're looking for reservoirs, you know."

They moved slowly down the metal avenue, between the twisted shadow shapes, looking carefully about them.

Rodney paused. "We might not recognize one."

Martin urged him on. "You know what a man-hole cover looks like." He added dryly, "Use your imagination."

They reached the metal wall at the end of the avenue and paused again, uncertain.

Martin swung his flashlight, illuminating the distorted metal shapes.

Wass said, "All this had a purpose, once...."

"We'll disperse and search carefully," Martin said.

"I wonder what the pattern was."

"... The reservoirs, Wass. The pattern will still be here for later expeditions to study. So will we if we don't find a way to get out."

Their radios recorded Rodney's gasp. Then—"Martin! Martin! I think I've found something!"

Martin began to run. After a moment's hesitation, Wass swung in behind him.

"Here," Rodney said, as they came up to him, out of breath. "Here. See? Right here."

Three flashlights centered on a dark, metal disk raised a foot or more from the floor.

"Well, they had hands." With his torch Wass indicated a small wheel of the same metal as everything else in the city, set beside the disk.

From its design Martin assumed that the disk was meant to be grasped and turned. He wondered what precisely they were standing over.

"Well, Skipper, are you going to do the honors?"

Martin kneeled, grasped the wheel. It turned easily—almost too easily—rotating the disk as it turned.

Suddenly, without a sound, the disk rose, like a hatch, on a concealed hinge.

The three men, clad in their suits and helmets, grouped around the six-foot opening, shining their torches down into the thing that drifted and eddied directly beneath them.

Rodney's sudden grip on Martin's wrist nearly shattered the bone. "Martin! It's all alive! It's moving!"

Martin hesitated long enough for a coil to move sinuously up toward the opening. Then he spun the wheel and the hatch slammed down.

He was shaking.

After a time he said, "Rodney, Wass, it's dust, down there. Remember the wind? Air currents are moving it."

Rodney sat down on the metal flooring. For a long time he said nothing. Then—"It wasn't.... Why did you close the hatch then?"

Martin did not say he thought the other two would have shot him, otherwise. He said merely, "At first I wasn't sure myself."

Rodney stood up, backing away from the closed hatch. He held his gun loosely, and his hand shook. "Then prove it. Open it again."

Martin went to the wheel. He noticed Wass was standing behind Rodney and he, too, had drawn his gun.

The hatch rose again at Martin's direction. He stood beside it, outlined in the light of two torches.

For a little while he was alone.

Then—causing a gasp from Wass, a harsh expletive from Rodney—a tenuous, questing alien limb edged through the hatch, curling about Martin, sparkling in ten thousand separate particles in the torchlight, obscuring the dimly seen backdrop of geometrical processions of strange objects.

Martin raised an arm, and the particles swirled in stately, shimmering spirals.

Rodney leaned forward and looked over the edge of the hatch. He said nothing. He eyed the sparkling particles swirling about Martin, and now, himself.

"How deep," Wass said, from his safe distance.

"We'll have to lower a flashlight," Martin answered.

Rodney, all eagerness to be of assistance now, lowered a rope with a torch swinging wildly on the end of it.

The torch came to rest about thirty feet down. It shone on gently rolling mounds of fine, white stuff.

Martin anchored the rope soundly, and paused, half across the lip of the hatch to stare coldly at Wass. "You'd rather monkey with the switches and blow yourself to smithereens?"

Wass sighed and refused to meet Martin's gaze. Martin looked at him disgustedly, and then began to descend the rope, slowly, peering into the infinite, sparkling darkness pressing around him. At the bottom of the rope he sank to his knees in dust, and then was held even. He stamped his feet, and then, as well as he was able, did a standing jump. He sank no farther than his knees.

He sighted a path parallel with the avenue above, toward the nearest edge of the city. "I think we'll be all right," he called out, "as long as we avoid the drifts."

Rodney began the descent. Looking up, Martin saw Wass above Rodney.

"All right, Wass," Martin said quietly, as Rodney released the rope and sank into the dust.

"Not me," the answer came back quickly. "You two fools go your way, I'll go mine."

"Wass!"

There was no answer. The light faded swiftly away from the opening.

The going was hard. The dust clung like honey to their feet, and eddied and swirled about them until the purifying systems in their suits were hard-pressed to remove the fine stuff working in at joints and valves.

"Are we going straight?" Rodney asked.

"Of course," Martin growled.

There was silence again, the silence of almost-exhausted determination. The two men lifted their feet out of the dust, and then laboriously plunged forward, to sink again to the knees, repeated the act, times without number.

Then Wass broke his silence, taunting. "The ship leaves in two hours, Martin. Two hours. Hear me, Rodney?"

Martin pulled his left foot from the sand and growled deep in his throat. Ahead, through the confusing patterns of the sparkling dust, his flashlight gleamed against metal. He grabbed Rodney's arm, pointed.

A grate.

Rodney stared. "Wass!" he shouted. "We've found a way out!"

Their radios recorded Wass' laughter. "I'm at the switchboard now, Martin. I—"

There was a tinkle of breaking glass, breaking faceplate.

The grate groaned upward and stopped.

Wass babbled incoherently into the radio for a moment, and then he began to scream.

Martin switched off his radio, sick.

He turned it on again when they reached the opening in the metal wall. "Well?"

"I've been trying to get you," Rodney said, frantically. "Why didn't you answer?"

"We couldn't do anything for him."

Rodney's face was white and drawn. "But he did this for us."

"So he did," Martin said, very quietly.

Rodney said nothing.

Then Martin said, "Did you listen until the end?"

Rodney nodded, jerkily. "He pulled three more switches. I couldn't understand it all. But—Martin, dying alone like that in a place like this—!"

Martin crawled into the circular pipe behind the grate. It tilted up toward the surface. "Come on, Rodney. Last lap."

An hour later they surfaced about two hundred yards away from the edge of the city. Behind them the black pile rose, the dome of force shimmering, almost invisible, about it.

Ahead of them were the other two scoutships from the mother ship. Martin called out faintly, pulling Rodney out of the pipe. Crew members standing by the scoutships, and at the edge of the city, began to run toward them.

"Radio picked you up as soon as you entered the pipe," someone said. It was the last thing Martin heard before he collapsed.

www.ingramcontent.com/pod-product-compliance
Lightning Source LLC
LaVergne TN
LVHW090857100726
842905LV00054B/420